WITHDRAWN

Welcome to Switzerland

By Pamela K. Harris
and Brad Clemmons

The
Child's
World®

Welcome to the WORLD

Published by The Child's World®
1980 Lookout Drive
Mankato, MN 56003-1705
800-599-READ
www.childsworld.com

Content Adviser: Dr. Charles Gichana Manyara, Associate Professor,
Department of Geography, Radford University, Radford, VA
Design and Production: The Creative Spark, San Juan Capistrano, CA
Editorial: Publisher's Diner, Wendy Mead, Greenwich, CT
Photo Research: Deborah Goodsite, Califon, NJ

Cover and title page photo: Jon Arnold Images/Alamy
Interior photos: Alamy: 10 (North Wind Picture Archives), 27 (mediacolor's); AP Photo: 16
(Keystone/fls), 17 (Keystone/Eddy Risch), 19 (Keystone/Arno Balzarini), 20 (Keystone/Martin
Ruetschi), 21 (Keystone/Sandro Campardo), 25 (Keystone/Walter Bieri); Corbis: 3 top, 15 (Adam
Woolfitt), 24 (Martin Ruetschi/Keystone); Getty Images: 11 (Jan Greune), 23 (Peter von Felbert/
LOOK), 26 (Tim Graham); iStockphoto.com: 3 bottom, 6 (Alan Tobey), 7 top (Peter Jobst), 7 bottom
(alohaspirit), 8 (zbindere), 22 (Colin Soutar), 28 (Ufuk Zivana), 29 (Michael Chen); Lonely Planet
Images: 13 (Glenn Beanland); NASA Earth Observatory: 4 (Reto Stockli); Photolibrary Group: 3
middle, 9, 14; Photo Researchers, Inc.: 30 (Paolo Koch).

Library of Congress Cataloging-in-Publication Data
Harris, Pamela K., 1962–
  Welcome to Switzerland / by Pamela K. Harris and Brad Clemmons.
      p. cm. — (Welcome to the world)
  Includes index.
  ISBN 978-1-59296-980-7 (library bound : alk. paper)
  1. Switzerland—Juvenile literature I. Clemmons, Brad. II. Title.
  III. Series.

  DQ17.H36 2008
  949.4—dc22
                                                                    2007038146

Printed in the United States of America
Mankato, Minnesota
September 2009
PA02022

Contents

Where Is Switzerland?

If you could see Earth from outer space, you would see large areas of land called **continents.** One land area is the largest of all. Its eastern part is called Asia, and its western part is called Europe. Switzerland is in Europe.

Switzerland is **landlocked,** which means that it has no seacoast. It is surrounded by five other countries.

France borders Switzerland to the north and west. Germany lies to the north, Austria and tiny Liechtenstein to the east, and Italy to the south.

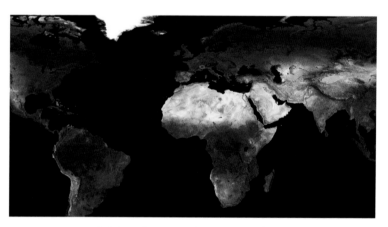

This picture gives us a flat look at Earth. Switzerland is inside the red circle.

Did you know?

The official name for Switzerland is "The Swiss Confederation."

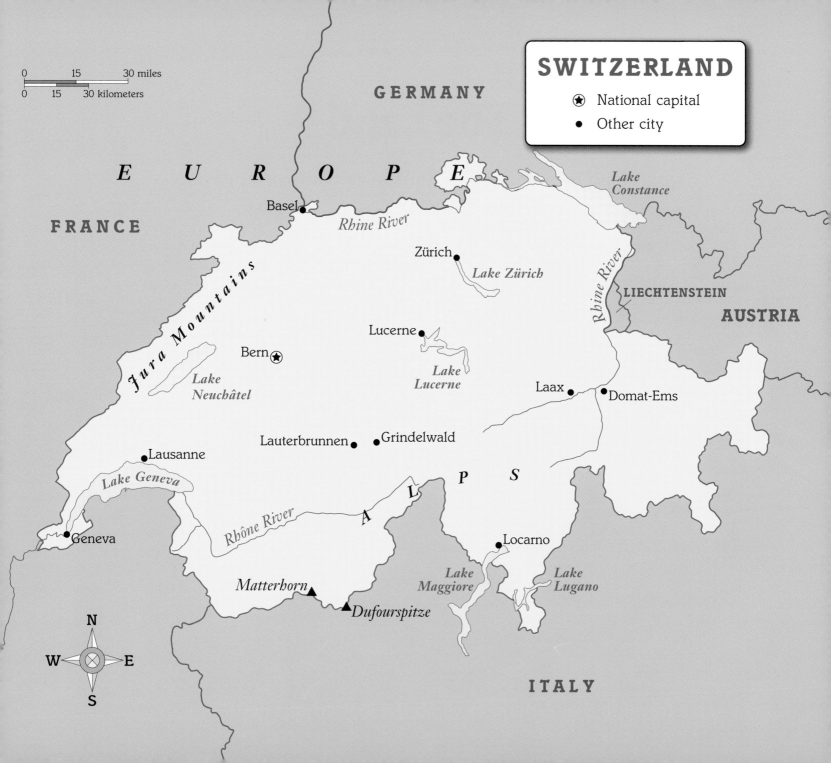

The Land

Switzerland is very mountainous, especially around its borders. The Jura (YOO-rah) Mountains are in the north and west, and the Alps are in the south and east. The Matterhorn, Switzerland's most famous mountain, is in the Alps. Switzerland's highest peak is Dufourspitze (doo-FOR-shpit-zeh), which stands 15,203 feet (4,634 meters) high.

Many people travel to Switzerland to climb the Matterhorn (left).

Central Switzerland is called the Mittelland, which is German for "middle land." This scenic area has rolling hills and views of beautiful mountains in the distance. It also has deep valleys with streams and roaring waterfalls. The weather in the central region is milder than in the snowcapped mountains.

A waterfall near Lauterbrunnen

Did you know?

Switzerland does not have any coastal areas. But it has several rivers, including the Rhine and the Rhône. Switzerland also has many lakes, including Lake Bachalpsee near Grindelwald shown here.

7

Cherry tree in bloom

Plants and Animals

Switzerland's plant life varies with the height of the land. Walnut, apple, pear, almond, and cherry trees grow on lower land. Higher in the mountains, pine and fir trees are more common. Above 10,000 feet (3,048 meters), the meadows are filled with edelweiss (AY-dul-vyss), alpenroses, and other wildflowers. Some wildflowers bloom for only one week every year.

The Alps are home to most of Switzerland's wildlife, including foxes and deer. There are also small antelopes called chamois (SHAM-ee) and a type of mountain goat called an ibex. Fish such as salmon and trout swim in Switzerland's streams and rivers.

The ibex is known for its long, ridged horns.

Long Ago

More than 30,000 years ago, most of Switzerland was covered with a thick sheet of ice that flowed down from the mountains. As the land warmed up, people began to settle in Switzerland. They learned to farm and fish in the river valleys. By 850 B.C.,

Members of the Helvetii tribe hold a meeting.

central Switzerland was controlled by the Helvetii, a powerful tribe of **Celts** (KELTS). Julius Caesar and the Romans conquered the Helvetii in 58 B.C. Almost 600 years later, the Romans were defeated by other tribes in the region.

Structures built by the Romans, such as this bridge, can still be seen in Switzerland today.

In 1291, different areas agreed to work together, establishing what became known as the Swiss Confederation. Later they wrote a **constitution,** or set of rules and laws. The Swiss Federal Constitution, modeled after the Constitution of the United States, was created in 1848. It balanced power and decision making between the federal and local governments.

Switzerland Today

Today Switzerland is known for its successes in business and banking. The nation's laws are made by a **parliament** of elected representatives and a council of seven key leaders. The country is divided into areas called **cantons,** which are like the states of the United States. Each canton has its own local government.

For hundreds of years the Swiss have practiced **neutrality**—refusing to take sides when other nations disagree. They maintained their neutrality during World War I and World War II. More recently, they have declined to join the European Union, a group of many European countries that work together.

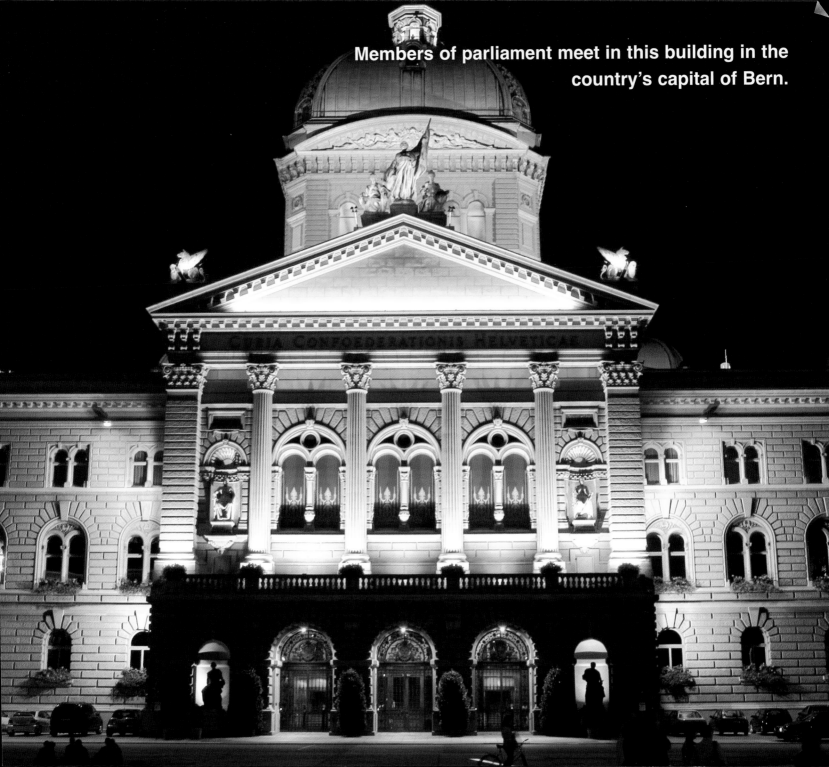

Members of parliament meet in this building in the country's capital of Bern.

The People

Switzerland has one of the most mixed populations in Europe. Many of the people, customs, and languages come from the neighboring lands of Germany, France, and Italy. One-fifth of the people are **immigrants** who have come from other parts of Europe. Switzerland also has immigrants from other areas of the world, including Africa, India, and Southeast Asia.

A father and daughter take a hike in Locarno near the border with Italy.

Most of Switzerland's people are Christians, either Roman Catholic or Protestant. The Protestant religion was formed centuries ago when a group of people split from the Catholic Church. The split led to some of Switzerland's worst fighting. Other religions practiced in Switzerland today include the Jewish, Islamic, and Greek Orthodox faiths.

A group of Christian children hold candles as part of a Christmas celebration.

Did you know?

Switzerland has been home to many scholars, scientists, and inventors. Swiss people invented products ranging from cellophane to dried soup to milk chocolate! One Swiss man noticed the burrs that stuck to his dog when they went for walks in the mountains. He copied the way the burrs worked and invented the Velcro® fastener!

15

A streetcar travels around Basel.

City Life and Country Life

Most of Switzerland's people live in cities or smaller towns. Zürich (ZUR-ik) is the largest city, with almost one million residents. Bern is the capital of Switzerland. In the cities, most people work in office buildings, shops, or banks. In the summer, they meet for coffee in outdoor cafes. Many people ride streetcars and trains to work instead of driving cars.

Although most of Switzerland has many mountains, few people live on them. In these areas, farmers raise dairy cows that produce milk and cheese. Other farmers grow grapes for making wine. Some farmers grow fruits for preserves and desserts. Country farmhouses are often decorated with giant cowbells.

A farmer wearing traditional clothing leads his cows to the meadows where they will spend the summer.

Schools and Language

Swiss children begin primary school at age six or seven and continue through grade nine. After that, they have two choices. They can either go to high school or take a *lehre* (LAY-reh). A lehre is an apprenticeship for learning a trade such as carpentry or plumbing.

Close to two-thirds of Switzerland's people speak a **dialect,** or type, of German called *Schwyzertütsch* (SHVY-tser-tootsh). People in Geneva and the west speak French. Italian is spoken in southern Switzerland. In all, the country has four main languages: German, French,

Students study Romansh at a school in Domat-Ems.

Italian, and Romansh (roh-MAHNCH). Romansh is a very old language spoken in the eastern-Alp area.

Many Swiss people know two, three, or even four languages. Sometimes when two people talk, each person is speaking a different language!

A worker puts away gold at the Swiss National Bank in Bern.

Work

Making watches is very challenging work.

More than half of Switzerland's people work in jobs that provide some kind of service for other people. Switzerland is an international banking center, which means people and businesses from all over the world use their banks. Many people work in banking-related jobs. Providing services for visitors is another important business.

In Switzerland, few people make their living from farming. Many more work in manufacturing. Swiss factories make machinery, chemicals, clothing, and food. Swiss-made clocks and watches are especially famous.

Food

Many Swiss foods borrow from German, French, and Italian cooking styles. Different regions of the country have different specialties. Among Switzerland's most famous foods are fine chocolate, wines, and *muesli* (MYOO-slee), a kind of whole-grain breakfast cereal.

Switzerland is also known for its cheeses. The best-known kind, Swiss cheese, is famous for its holes!

Gruyère (groo-YAYR) and Emmentaler (EM-en-tall-er) cheeses are melted together to make a famous Swiss dish called *fondue* (fon-DOO). To eat fondue, people put pieces of bread on long-handled forks and dip them

Cheese *fondue*

A family celebrates Christmas together with a special holiday meal.

into the melted cheese. *Raclette* (rah-KLET) is another favorite dish. It is simply melted cheese that is often served over potatoes.

Children learn to ski at Wengen, one of Switzerland's best-known ski resorts.

Pastimes

People in Switzerland enjoy such sports as hiking and biking. During the winter, skiing and snowboarding on the country's many mountains is another way the Swiss like to spend their time. In the summer, people play in the waters of lakes and rivers. They also love to read, golf, play tennis, listen to music, and hang out with family and friends.

People cool off in the waters of Cresta Lake near the city of Laax.

Holidays

A person dresses in costume for a winter festival.

On August 1, people celebrate Swiss National Day. It marks the day when the Swiss Confederation was formed in 1291. There are lots of fireworks and barbeques—much like the Fourth of July in the United States.

For the Swiss, Christmas starts a little bit early. On December 6, St. Nicholas visits children and leaves small presents in their shoes. Families also gather together on Christmas Eve to celebrate and enjoy their beautifully decorated Christmas trees.

Crowds flock to Lake Lucerne to celebrate Swiss National Day.

Fast Facts About Switzerland

Area: About 16,000 square miles (41,000 square kilometers)—about twice as big as Massachusetts

Population: Over 7 million people

Capital City: Bern

Other Important Cities: Zürich, Geneva, Basel, and Lausanne

Important Rivers: The Rhine and the Rhône

Heads of Government: The president and the Bundesrat of Switzerland. The Bundesrat is a federal council made up of seven members.

Money: The Swiss franc (FRANHK), which is divided into 100 centimes (SAHN-teem), called rappen (RAHP-pen) in the German regions

National Holiday: National Day, August 1

National Flag: A white cross on a red background. The cross originally stood for the Christian religion, but now it also represents Switzerland's neutrality. The flag of the International Red Cross is modeled after the Swiss flag.

Famous People:

Werner Arber: Nobel Prize-winning scientist

Henry Dunant: co-founder of the International Committee of the Red Cross

Martina Hingis: tennis player

Carl Spitteler: poet

Johanna Spyri: children's book author

Kurt Wüthrich: Nobel Prize-winning chemist

National Song: "Swiss Psalm"

When the morning skies grow red
And o'er us their radiance shed,
Thou, O Lord, appeareth in their light.
When the Alps grow bright with splendor,
Pray to God, to Him surrender,
For you feel and understand,
For you feel and understand,
That He dwelleth in this land.
That He dwelleth in this land.

In the sunset Thou art nigh
And beyond the starry sky,
Thou, O loving Father, ever near.
When to Heaven we are departing,
Joy and bliss Thou'lt be imparting,

For we feel and understand,
For we feel and understand,
That Thou dwelleth in this land.
That Thou dwelleth in this land.

When dark clouds enshroud the hills
And gray mist the valley fills,
Yet Thou art not hidden from Thy sons.
Pierce the gloom in which we cower
With Thy sunshine's cleansing power
Then we'll feel and understand
Then we'll feel and understand
That God dwelleth in this land.
That God dwelleth in this land.

Swiss Folktale:

Switzerland is famous for its Saint Bernards, a type of rescue dog. These dogs take their name from Saint Bernard, a man who built rest areas and gave shelter to travelers in the Alps. He established his first place on what is now called Great Saint Bernard Pass around 967. A short time later, Saint Bernard created another shelter on what is now Little Saint Bernard Pass. Sometime around the 1600s, large, shaggy dogs were brought to these places and trained to help travelers in trouble. For hundreds of years, Saint Bernards have saved numerous people who have been lost out in the cold, snowy mountains.

How Do You Say...

ENGLISH	GERMAN	HOW TO SAY IT
Hello	grüezi	groo-UT-see
Good-bye	auf widerseden	AUF VEE-der-zayn
Please	bitte	BIT-teh
Thank You	danke	DAN-kuh
One	eins	EYNTS
Two	zwei	tSVY
Three	drei	DRY
Switzerland	Schweiz	SHVYTZ

cantons (KAN-tonz) Cantons are states or areas within a country. Switzerland has more than twenty cantons.

Celts (KELTS) The Celts were a group of people who lived in Europe thousands of years ago. Central Switzerland was once controlled by a tribe of Celts called the Helvetii.

constitution (kon-stuh-TOO-shun) A constitution is a written set of a government's rules and beliefs. Switzerland created its first constitution in 1848.

continents (KON-tih-nents) Earth's continents are huge land areas surrounded mostly by water. Switzerland is on the continent of Europe.

dialect (DY-uh-lekt) A dialect is a different form of a language that is spoken in a particular region or by a particular group. Many Swiss people speak a dialect of German.

immigrants (IM-ih-grents) Immigrants are people who move to a land from somewhere else. Switzerland has immigrants from other nations in Europe and around the world.

landlocked (LAND-lokt) A landlocked country is surrounded by land rather than being next to an ocean or sea. Switzerland is landlocked.

neutrality (noo-TRAL-ih-tee) Being neutral is avoiding taking a side in a war or political conflict. Switzerland follows a policy of neutrality in international affairs.

parliament (PAR-leh-ment) A parliament is a group of elected leaders that make a nation's laws. Switzerland has a parliament.

31

Further Information

Read It

Foley, Ronan. *The Rhine*. Chicago: Raintree, 2004.

Harvey, Miles. *Look What Came from Switzerland*. Danbury, CT: Franklin Watts, 2002.

Hughes, Helga, Robert L. Wolfe, and Diana Wolfe. *Cooking the Swiss Way*. Minneapolis, MN: Lerner Publications, 1995.

Somervill, Barbara A. *The Awesome Alps*. Chanhassen, MN: The Child's World, 2005.

Look It Up

Visit our Web page for lots of links about Switzerland:
http://www.childsworld.com/links

Note to Parents, Teachers, and Librarians: We routinely verify our Web links to make sure they are safe, active sites—so encourage your readers to check them out!

Index